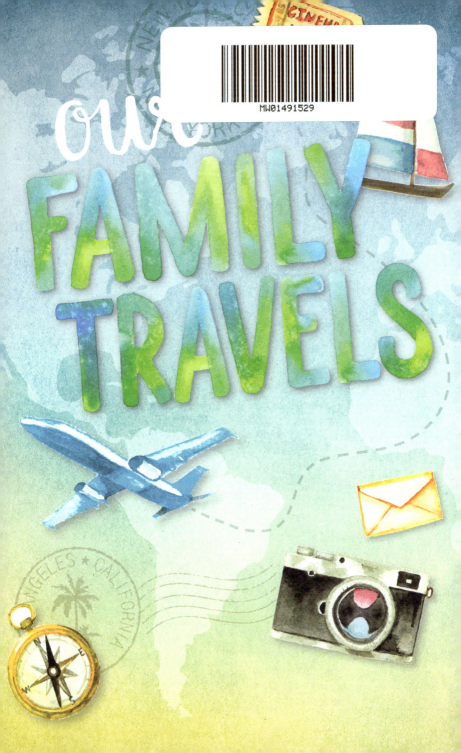

our FAMILY TRAVELS

ISBN-13: 978-1-56383-593-3
Item #5601

Printed in the USA   www.cqbookstore.com

Distributed By: gifts@cqbookstore.com

507 Industrial Street
Waverly, IA 50677

 CQ Products

 CQ Products

 @cqproducts

 @cqproducts

You have the journal, now what?

IT'S EASY! CREATE THIS KEEPSAKE ANY WAY THAT WORKS WELL FOR YOUR FAMILY. HERE ARE A FEW IDEAS TO GET YOU STARTED:

★ GET EVERYONE INVOLVED TO MAKE IT A FAMILY ACTIVITY.

★ TAKE A FEW MINUTES EVERY EVENING TO RECALL AND RECORD THE DAY'S MOST MEMORABLE MOMENTS.

★ FOLLOW THE SIMPLE PROMPTS OR GO ROGUE – JUST HAVE FUN AND MAKE IT YOUR OWN.

★ TAKE ALONG ON EVERY OUTING SO YOU DON'T FORGET A SINGLE DETAIL!

Go Make Some Memories!

Today's Adventures

date .... location ....

weather ☐ ☀ ☐ ⛅ ☐ ☁ ☐ 🌧 ☐ 💨 ☐ ❄

rating ☐ AWESOME ☐ GOOD ☐ SO-SO ☐ NOT SO GOOD ☐ UGH!

Quick Details

WHAT WE DID TODAY

FAVORITE PART OF THE DAY

WORST THING ABOUT TODAY

BEST THING WE ATE & WHERE

People we met

Strangest thing we saw or did

Discoveries

_____

_____

_____

_____

_____

_____

_____

_____

_____

_____

This made us laugh

_____

_____

_____

_____

_____

_____

_____

_____

_____

Things we need more space to write about

Today's Adventures

date _____ location _____

weather ☐ ☀ ☐ ⛅ ☐ ☁ ☐ 🌧 ☐ 🌬 ☐ ❄

rating ☐ AWESOME ☐ GOOD ☐ SO-SO ☐ NOT SO GOOD ☐ UGH!

Quick Details

WHAT WE DID TODAY _____
_____
_____

FAVORITE PART OF THE DAY _____
_____
_____

WORST THING ABOUT TODAY _____
_____
_____

BEST THING WE ATE & WHERE _____
_____
_____

People we met
_____
_____
_____

Strangest thing we saw or did

Things we need more space to write about

Discoveries

This made us laugh

Today's Adventures

date _____ **location** _____

weather ☐ ☀ ☐ ⛅ ☐ ☁ ☐ 🌧 ☐ 🌬 ☐ ❄

rating ☐ AWESOME ☐ GOOD ☐ SO-SO ☐ NOT SO GOOD ☐ UGH!

Quick Details

WHAT WE DID TODAY _____

FAVORITE PART OF THE DAY _____

WORST THING ABOUT TODAY _____

BEST THING WE ATE & WHERE _____

People we met

Strangest thing we saw or did

Discoveries

This made us laugh

Things we need more space to write about

Today's Adventures

date .... location

weather ☐ ☀ ☐ ⛅ ☐ ☁ ☐ 🌧 ☐ 🌬 ☐ ❄

rating ☐ AWESOME ☐ GOOD ☐ SO-SO ☐ NOT SO GOOD ☐ UGH!

Quick Details

WHAT WE DID TODAY

FAVORITE PART OF THE DAY

WORST THING ABOUT TODAY

BEST THING WE ATE & WHERE

People we met

Strangest thing we saw or did

Discoveries

This made us laugh

Things we need more space to write about

Today's Adventures

date _____ **location** _____

weather ☐ ☀ ☐ ⛅ ☐ ☁ ☐ 🌧 ☐ 🌬 ☐ ❄

rating ☐ AWESOME ☐ GOOD ☐ SO-SO ☐ NOT SO GOOD ☐ UGH!

Quick Details

WHAT WE DID TODAY _____

_____

_____

FAVORITE PART OF THE DAY

_____

_____

WORST THING ABOUT TODAY

_____

_____

BEST THING WE ATE & WHERE

_____

_____

People we met

_____

_____

_____

_____

Strangest thing we saw or did

Things we need more space to write about

Discoveries

▽
▽
▽
▽
▽
▽
▽
▽
▽
▽
▽
▽
▽
▽

This made us laugh

Today's Adventures

date _____ location _____

weather ☐ ☀ ☐ ⛅ ☐ ☁ ☐ 🌧 ☐ 🌬 ☐ ❄

rating ☐ AWESOME ☐ GOOD ☐ SO-SO ☐ NOT SO GOOD ☐ UGH!

Quick Details

WHAT WE DID TODAY _____

_____

_____

FAVORITE PART OF THE DAY _____

_____

_____

WORST THING ABOUT TODAY _____

_____

_____

BEST THING WE ATE & WHERE _____

_____

People we met

_____

_____

_____

_____

Strangest thing we saw or did

Things we need more space to write about

Discoveries

▽
▽
▽
▽
▽
▽
▽
▽
▽
▽
▽
▽
▽
▽
▽

This made us laugh

Today's Adventures

date _____ **location** _____

weather ☐ ☀ ☐ ⛅ ☐ ☁ ☐ 🌧 ☐ 🌬 ☐ ❄

rating ☐ AWESOME ☐ GOOD ☐ SO-SO ☐ NOT SO GOOD ☐ UGH!

Quick Details

WHAT WE DID TODAY
_____
_____
_____

FAVORITE PART OF THE DAY
_____
_____
_____

WORST THING ABOUT TODAY
_____
_____
_____

BEST THING WE ATE & WHERE
_____
_____
_____

People we met
_____
_____
_____
_____

Strangest thing we saw or did

Discoveries

This made us laugh

Things we need more space to write about

Today's Adventures

date _____ **location** _____

weather ☐ ☀ ☐ ⛅ ☐ ☁ ☐ 🌧 ☐ 🌬 ☐ ❄

rating ☐ AWESOME ☐ GOOD ☐ SO-SO ☐ NOT SO GOOD ☐ UGH!

Quick Details

WHAT WE DID TODAY _____
_____
_____
_____

FAVORITE PART OF THE DAY _____
_____
_____
_____

WORST THING ABOUT TODAY _____
_____
_____

BEST THING WE ATE & WHERE _____
_____
_____
_____

People we met
_____
_____
_____
_____

Strangest thing we saw or did

Discoveries   This made us laugh

Things we need more space to write about

Today's Adventures

date _____   **location** _____

weather ☐ ☀ ☐ ⛅ ☐ ☁ ☐ 🌧 ☐ 🌬 ☐ ❄

rating ☐ AWESOME   ☐ GOOD   ☐ SO-SO   ☐ NOT SO GOOD   ☐ UGH!

Quick Details

WHAT WE DID TODAY _____

_____

FAVORITE PART OF THE DAY _____

_____

WORST THING ABOUT TODAY _____

_____

BEST THING WE ATE & WHERE _____

_____

People we met

_____

_____

_____

_____

Strangest thing we saw or did

Discoveries

This made us laugh

Things we need more space to write about

Today's Adventures

date _____ **location** _____

weather ☐ ☀ ☐ ⛅ ☐ ☁ ☐ 🌧 ☐ 🌬 ☐ ❄

rating ☐ AWESOME ☐ GOOD ☐ SO-SO ☐ NOT SO GOOD ☐ UGH!

Quick Details

WHAT WE DID TODAY
_____
_____

FAVORITE PART OF THE DAY
_____
_____

WORST THING ABOUT TODAY
_____
_____

BEST THING WE ATE & WHERE
_____
_____

People we met
_____
_____
_____

Strangest thing we saw or did

Things we need more space to write about

Discoveries

This made us laugh

Today's Adventures

date _____ **location** _____

weather ☐ ☀ ☐ ⛅ ☐ ☁ ☐ 🌧 ☐ 🌬 ☐ ❄

rating ☐ AWESOME ☐ GOOD ☐ SO-SO ☐ NOT SO GOOD ☐ UGH!

Quick Details

WHAT WE DID TODAY

FAVORITE PART OF THE DAY

WORST THING ABOUT TODAY

BEST THING WE ATE & WHERE

People we met

Strangest thing we saw or did

Discoveries

This made us laugh

Things we need more space to write about

Today's Adventures

date .... **location** ....

weather ☐ ☀ ☐ ⛅ ☐ ☁ ☐ 🌧 ☐ 🌬 ☐ ❄

rating ☐ AWESOME ☐ GOOD ☐ SO-SO ☐ NOT SO GOOD ☐ UGH!

Quick Details

WHAT WE DID TODAY ....

FAVORITE PART OF THE DAY

WORST THING ABOUT TODAY

BEST THING WE ATE & WHERE

People we met

Strangest thing we saw or did

Discoveries

This made us laugh

Things we need more space to write about

Today's Adventures

date

location

weather ☐ ☀ ☐ ⛅ ☐ ☁ ☐ 🌧 ☐ 🌬 ☐ ❄

rating ☐ AWESOME ☐ GOOD ☐ SO-SO ☐ NOT SO GOOD ☐ UGH!

Quick Details

WHAT WE DID TODAY

FAVORITE PART OF THE DAY

WORST THING ABOUT TODAY

BEST THING WE ATE & WHERE

People we met

Strangest thing we saw or did

Discoveries

This made us laugh

Things we need more space to write about

Today's Adventures

date _____ **location** _____

weather ☐ ☼ ☐ ⛅ ☐ ☁ ☐ 🌧 ☐ 🌬 ☐ ❄

rating ☐ AWESOME ☐ GOOD ☐ SO-SO ☐ NOT SO GOOD ☐ UGH!

Quick Details

WHAT WE DID TODAY _____

_____

_____

FAVORITE PART OF THE DAY _____

_____

_____

WORST THING ABOUT TODAY _____

_____

_____

BEST THING WE ATE & WHERE _____

_____

Strangest thing we saw or did

People we met

_____

_____

_____

_____

Things we need more space to write about

Discoveries

▽
▽
▽
▽
▽
▽
▽
▽
▽
▽
▽
▽
▽
▽
▽

This made us laugh

Today's Adventures

date .... **location** ....

weather ☐ ☀ ☐ ⛅ ☐ ☁ ☐ 🌧 ☐ 💨 ☐ ❄

rating ☐ AWESOME ☐ GOOD ☐ SO-SO ☐ NOT SO GOOD ☐ UGH!

Quick Details

WHAT WE DID TODAY

FAVORITE PART OF THE DAY

WORST THING ABOUT TODAY

BEST THING WE ATE & WHERE

Strangest thing we saw or did

People we met

Discoveries

_____

_____

_____

_____

_____

_____

_____

_____

_____

_____

_____

This made us laugh

_____

_____

_____

_____

_____

_____

_____

_____

Things we need more space to write about

Today's Adventures

date

location

weather ☐ ☀ ☐ ⛅ ☐ ☁ ☐ 🌧 ☐ 🌬 ☐ ❄

rating ☐ AWESOME ☐ GOOD ☐ SO-SO ☐ NOT SO GOOD ☐ UGH!

Quick Details

WHAT WE DID TODAY

FAVORITE PART OF THE DAY

WORST THING ABOUT TODAY

BEST THING WE ATE & WHERE

People we met

Strangest thing we saw or did

Discoveries

This made us laugh

Things we need more space to write about

Today's Adventures

date _____ **location** _____

weather ☐ ☀ ☐ ⛅ ☐ ☁ ☐ 🌧 ☐ 🌬 ☐ ❄

rating ☐ AWESOME ☐ GOOD ☐ SO-SO ☐ NOT SO GOOD ☐ UGH!

Quick Details

WHAT WE DID TODAY _____

_____

_____

FAVORITE PART OF THE DAY _____

_____

_____

WORST THING ABOUT TODAY _____

_____

_____

BEST THING WE ATE & WHERE _____

_____

_____

People we met

_____

_____

_____

Strangest thing we saw or did

Things we need more space to write about

Discoveries

This made us laugh

Today's Adventures

date   location

weather   ☐ ☀   ☐ ⛅   ☐ ☁   ☐ 🌧   ☐ 🌬   ☐ ❄

rating   ☐ AWESOME   ☐ GOOD   ☐ SO-SO   ☐ NOT SO GOOD   ☐ UGH!

Quick Details

WHAT WE DID TODAY

FAVORITE PART OF THE DAY

WORST THING ABOUT TODAY

BEST THING WE ATE & WHERE

People we met

Strangest thing we saw or did

Discoveries

This made us laugh

Things we need more space to write about

Today's Adventures

date _____ **location** _____

weather ☐ ☀ ☐ ⛅ ☐ ☁ ☐ 🌧 ☐ 🌬 ☐ ❄

rating ☐ AWESOME ☐ GOOD ☐ SO-SO ☐ NOT SO GOOD ☐ UGH!

Quick Details

WHAT WE DID TODAY _____

_____

_____

FAVORITE PART OF THE DAY _____

_____

_____

WORST THING ABOUT TODAY _____

_____

_____

BEST THING WE ATE & WHERE _____

_____

_____

People we met

_____

_____

_____

_____

Strangest thing we saw or did

Things we need more space to write about

Discoveries

▽
▽
▽
▽
▽
▽
▽
▽
▽
▽
▽
▽
▽
▽
▽

This made us laugh

Today's Adventures

date _____ location _____

weather ☐ ☀ ☐ ⛅ ☐ ☁ ☐ ⛈ ☐ 🌬 ☐ ❄

rating ☐ AWESOME ☐ GOOD ☐ SO-SO ☐ NOT SO GOOD ☐ UGH!

Quick Details

WHAT WE DID TODAY _____

FAVORITE PART OF THE DAY _____

WORST THING ABOUT TODAY _____

BEST THING WE ATE & WHERE _____

People we met

Strangest thing we saw or did

Discoveries

This made us laugh

Things we need more space to write about

Today's Adventures

date .... location ....

weather ☐ ☀ ☐ ⛅ ☐ ☁ ☐ 🌧 ☐ 🌬 ☐ ❄

rating ☐ AWESOME ☐ GOOD ☐ SO-SO ☐ NOT SO GOOD ☐ UGH!

Quick Details

WHAT WE DID TODAY

FAVORITE PART OF THE DAY

WORST THING ABOUT TODAY

BEST THING WE ATE & WHERE

People we met

Strangest thing we saw or did

Discoveries

This made us laugh

Things we need more space to write about

Today's Adventures

date _____ **location** _____

weather ☐ ☀ ☐ ⛅ ☐ ☁ ☐ 🌧 ☐ 🌬 ☐ ❄

rating ☐ AWESOME ☐ GOOD ☐ SO-SO ☐ NOT SO GOOD ☐ UGH!

Quick Details

WHAT WE DID TODAY _____

_____

FAVORITE PART OF THE DAY _____

_____

WORST THING ABOUT TODAY _____

_____

BEST THING WE ATE & WHERE _____

_____

Strangest thing we saw or did

People we met _____

_____

Things we need more space to write about

Discoveries

▽
▽
▽
▽
▽
▽

▽
▽
▽
▽
▽

▽
▽
▽
▽

This made us laugh

Today's Adventures

date .... **location** ....

weather ☐ ☀ ☐ ⛅ ☐ ☁ ☐ 🌧 ☐ 💨 ☐ ❄

rating ☐ AWESOME   ☐ GOOD   ☐ SO-SO   ☐ NOT SO GOOD   ☐ UGH!

Quick Details

WHAT WE DID TODAY

FAVORITE PART OF THE DAY

WORST THING ABOUT TODAY

BEST THING WE ATE & WHERE

People we met

Strangest thing we saw or did

Discoveries

This made us laugh

Things we need more space to write about

Today's Adventures

date _____ **location** _____

weather ☐ ☀ ☐ ⛅ ☐ ☁ ☐ 🌧 ☐ 🌬 ☐ ❄

rating ☐ AWESOME ☐ GOOD ☐ SO-SO ☐ NOT SO GOOD ☐ UGH!

Quick Details

WHAT WE DID TODAY _____

FAVORITE PART OF THE DAY _____

WORST THING ABOUT TODAY _____

BEST THING WE ATE & WHERE _____

People we met _____

Strangest thing we saw or did

Discoveries

This made us laugh

Things we need more space to write about

Today's Adventures

date _____ **location** _____

weather ☐ ☀ ☐ ⛅ ☐ ☁ ☐ 🌧 ☐ 🌬 ☐ ❄

rating ☐ AWESOME ☐ GOOD ☐ SO-SO ☐ NOT SO GOOD ☐ UGH!

Quick Details

WHAT WE DID TODAY
_____
_____
_____

FAVORITE PART OF THE DAY
_____
_____
_____

WORST THING ABOUT TODAY
_____
_____
_____

BEST THING WE ATE & WHERE
_____
_____
_____

People we met
_____
_____
_____
_____

Strangest thing we saw or did

Things we need more space to write about

Discoveries

▽
▽
▽
▽
▽
▽
▽
▽
▽
▽
▽
▽
▽
▽

This made us laugh

Today's Adventures

date .... location ....

weather ☐ ☀ ☐ ⛅ ☐ ☁ ☐ 🌧 ☐ 💨 ☐ ❄

rating ☐ AWESOME ☐ GOOD ☐ SO-SO ☐ NOT SO GOOD ☐ UGH!

Quick Details

WHAT WE DID TODAY

FAVORITE PART OF THE DAY

WORST THING ABOUT TODAY

BEST THING WE ATE & WHERE

People we met

Strangest thing we saw or did

Discoveries

This made us laugh

Things we need more space to write about

Today's Adventures

date _____ location _____

weather ☐ ☀ ☐ ⛅ ☐ ☁ ☐ 🌧 ☐ 🌬 ☐ ❄

rating ☐ AWESOME   ☐ GOOD   ☐ SO-SO   ☐ NOT SO GOOD   ☐ UGH!

Quick Details

WHAT WE DID TODAY

FAVORITE PART OF THE DAY

WORST THING ABOUT TODAY

BEST THING WE ATE & WHERE

Strangest thing we saw or did

People we met

Things we need more space to write about

Discoveries

▽
▽
▽
▽
▽
▽
▽
▽
▽
▽
▽
▽
▽
▽
▽

This made us laugh

Today's Adventures

date .... location ....

weather □ ☀ □ ⛅ □ ☁ □ 🌧 □ 🌬 □ ❄

rating □ AWESOME □ GOOD □ SO-SO □ NOT SO GOOD □ UGH!

Quick Details

WHAT WE DID TODAY ....

FAVORITE PART OF THE DAY ....

WORST THING ABOUT TODAY ....

BEST THING WE ATE & WHERE ....

People we met

Strangest thing we saw or did

Discoveries

This made us laugh

Things we need more space to write about

Today's Adventures

date _____ **location** _____

weather ☐ ☀ ☐ ⛅ ☐ ☁ ☐ 🌧 ☐ 🌬 ☐ ❄

rating ☐ AWESOME ☐ GOOD ☐ SO-SO ☐ NOT SO GOOD ☐ UGH!

Quick Details

WHAT WE DID TODAY _____

FAVORITE PART OF THE DAY _____

WORST THING ABOUT TODAY _____

BEST THING WE ATE & WHERE _____

People we met

_____

Strangest thing we saw or did

Discoveries

This made us laugh

Things we need more space to write about

Today's Adventures

date _____ **location** _____

weather ☐ ☀ ☐ ⛅ ☐ ☁ ☐ 🌧 ☐ 🌬 ☐ ❄

rating ☐ AWESOME ☐ GOOD ☐ SO-SO ☐ NOT SO GOOD ☐ UGH!

Quick Details

WHAT WE DID TODAY _____
_____
_____
_____

FAVORITE PART OF THE DAY _____
_____
_____
_____

WORST THING ABOUT TODAY _____
_____
_____
_____

BEST THING WE ATE & WHERE _____
_____
_____
_____

People we met

_____
_____
_____
_____

Strangest thing we saw or did

Discoveries

This made us laugh

Things we need more space to write about

Today's Adventures

date   location

weather   ☐ ☀   ☐ ⛅   ☐ ☁   ☐ 🌧   ☐ 🌬   ☐ ❄

rating   ☐ AWESOME   ☐ GOOD   ☐ SO-SO   ☐ NOT SO GOOD   ☐ UGH!

Quick Details

WHAT WE DID TODAY

FAVORITE PART OF THE DAY

WORST THING ABOUT TODAY

BEST THING WE ATE & WHERE

People we met

Strangest thing we saw or did

Things we need more space to write about

Discoveries

▽
▽
▽
▽
▽
▽
▽
▽
▽
▽
▽
▽
▽
▽

This made us laugh

Today's Adventures

date .... location ....

weather ☐ ☀ ☐ ⛅ ☐ ☁ ☐ 🌧 ☐ 🌬 ☐ ❄

rating ☐ AWESOME ☐ GOOD ☐ SO-SO ☐ NOT SO GOOD ☐ UGH!

Quick Details

WHAT WE DID TODAY

FAVORITE PART OF THE DAY

WORST THING ABOUT TODAY

BEST THING WE ATE & WHERE

People we met

Strangest thing we saw or did

Discoveries

This made us laugh

Things we need more space to write about

Today's Adventures

date _____ **location** _____

weather ☐ ☀ ☐ ⛅ ☐ ☁ ☐ 🌧 ☐ 🌬 ☐ ❄

rating ☐ AWESOME ☐ GOOD ☐ SO-SO ☐ NOT SO GOOD ☐ UGH!

Quick Details

WHAT WE DID TODAY
_____
_____
_____

FAVORITE PART OF THE DAY
_____
_____
_____

WORST THING ABOUT TODAY
_____
_____
_____

BEST THING WE ATE & WHERE
_____
_____
_____

People we met
_____
_____
_____
_____

Strangest thing we saw or did

Discoveries

This made us laugh

_____
_____
_____
_____
_____
_____
_____
_____

Things we need more space to write about

Today's Adventures

date _____ **location** _____

weather ☐ ☀ ☐ ⛅ ☐ ☁ ☐ 🌧 ☐ 🌬 ☐ ❄

rating ☐ AWESOME   ☐ GOOD   ☐ SO-SO   ☐ NOT SO GOOD   ☐ UGH!

Quick Details

WHAT WE DID TODAY _____

FAVORITE PART OF THE DAY _____

WORST THING ABOUT TODAY _____

BEST THING WE ATE & WHERE _____

People we met

Strangest thing we saw or did

Things we need more space to write about

Discoveries

▽
▽
▽
▽
▽
▽
▽
▽
▽
▽
▽
▽
▽
▽
▽

This made us laugh

Today's Adventures

date _____   **location** _____

weather ☐ ☀ ☐ ⛅ ☐ ☁ ☐ 🌧 ☐ 🌬 ☐ ❄

rating ☐ AWESOME ☐ GOOD ☐ SO-SO ☐ NOT SO GOOD ☐ UGH!

Quick Details

WHAT WE DID TODAY

FAVORITE PART OF THE DAY

WORST THING ABOUT TODAY

BEST THING WE ATE & WHERE

People we met

Strangest thing we saw or did

Discoveries

This made us laugh

Things we need more space to write about

Today's Adventures

date _____ **location** _____

weather ☐ ☀ ☐ ⛅ ☐ ☁ ☐ 🌧 ☐ 🌬 ☐ ❄

rating ☐ AWESOME ☐ GOOD ☐ SO-SO ☐ NOT SO GOOD ☐ UGH!

Quick Details

WHAT WE DID TODAY

_____

_____

_____

FAVORITE PART OF THE DAY

_____

_____

_____

WORST THING ABOUT TODAY

_____

_____

_____

BEST THING WE ATE & WHERE

_____

_____

_____

People we met

_____

_____

_____

Strangest thing we saw or did

Things we need more space to write about

Discoveries

▽
▽
▽
▽
▽
▽
▽
▽
▽
▽
▽
▽
▽
▽
▽

This made us laugh

Today's Adventures

date _____   location _____

weather ☐ ☀️ ☐ ⛅ ☐ ☁️ ☐ 🌧️ ☐ 💨 ☐ ❄️

rating ☐ AWESOME   ☐ GOOD   ☐ SO-SO   ☐ NOT SO GOOD   ☐ UGH!

Quick Details

WHAT WE DID TODAY _____

FAVORITE PART OF THE DAY _____

WORST THING ABOUT TODAY _____

BEST THING WE ATE & WHERE _____

People we met

_____

Strangest thing we saw or did

Discoveries

This made us laugh

Things we need more space to write about

Today's Adventures

date _____ **location** _____

weather ☐ ☀ ☐ ⛅ ☐ ☁ ☐ 🌧 ☐ 🌬 ☐ ❄

rating ☐ AWESOME ☐ GOOD ☐ SO-SO ☐ NOT SO GOOD ☐ UGH!

Quick Details

WHAT WE DID TODAY _____

_____

FAVORITE PART OF THE DAY _____

_____

WORST THING ABOUT TODAY _____

_____

BEST THING WE ATE & WHERE _____

_____

People we met _____

_____

_____

Strangest thing we saw or did

Things we need more space to write about

Discoveries

▽
▽
▽
▽
▽
▽
▽
▽
▽
▽
▽
▽
▽
▽
▽

This made us laugh

NOW THAT YOUR JOURNAL HAS BEEN FILLED WITH TRAVEL MEMORIES, LOOK BACK WITH YOUR FAMILY...

OVERALL, WHAT WAS YOUR FAVORITE TRIP IN THIS BOOK?

OF ALL THE SINGLE MEMORIES YOU'VE WRITTEN ABOUT, WHICH ONE IS THE BEST?

WHICH ACTIVITIES WOULD YOU LIKE TO DO AGAIN SOMEDAY?

WHICH MEMORY HAS YOU LAUGHING RIGHT NOW?

WHEN YOU THINK ABOUT ALL THE GREAT FOOD YOU ATE, WHAT MAKES YOUR MOUTH WATER, EVEN NOW?

ARE YOU STILL IN CONTACT WITH ANY OF THE PEOPLE YOU MET?

IF SO, WHO?

WHERE DO YOU WANT TO GO ON YOUR NEXT OUTING?

We didn't realize we were making memories,
we just knew we were having fun.